WHO AM I?

**Reflections on Self by the
Self-Satisfied, Self-Seeking and Self-Aware**

Compiled by Emily Rosen M.A., M.S.

Published by TriMark Press, Inc., Deerfield Beach, Florida.

Cover design by Allison C.M.

Library of Congress Cataloging-in-Publication Data
Who Am I by Emily Rosen and Various writers
p. cm.
ISBN: 978-1-943401-58-1
Library of Congress Control Number: 2019939210
D19
10 9 8 7 6 5 4 3 2 1
First Edition
Printed and Bound in the United States of America

A publication of TriMark Press, Inc.
368 South Military Trail
Deerfield Beach, FL 33442
800.889.0693
www.TriMarkPress.com

DEDICATION

To: All the people who promised to send me their "Who Am I" but had an interesting variety of excuses for never having done it.

To: Those who sent me their "Who Am I" but didn't want their work seen in print.

To: To those who refused unequivocally to tackle the project, for reasons best known to themselves, despite a very lax deadline.

AND MOSTLY

To: To those represented in these pages who thoughtfully and coura-geously – and in some cases somewhat surrealistically tackled this as a worthwhile project.

Organization of this Book

To what extent is one's vision of self, static? Or more to the point, are there some elements of self which are so defining that they never change? As you read through these, you may come to your own conclusion. As I read through them, each many times, it occurred to me that the most telling way to categorize this collection is by level of chronological maturity, perhaps giving us a clue as to how we change over a lifetime. Or, indeed, as in many cases herein—no clue at all.

Needless to say, chronological maturity is by no means a calculator of emotional, intellectual or spiritual maturity. Nor is "maturity" necessarily a hallmark of the true core of a person. But, with the necessity of having to organize this in some thoughtful way—this is what you will get: a collection of essays and thoughts from people organized by birth decade.

How do older people see themselves as they reflect on many years of past experience? How do younger people see themselves as they anticipate a future?

These essays were written at the end of 2017 (November and December) and sometime in 2018.

TABLE OF CONTENTS

Introduction

People have been writing "WHO AM I" essays since the quill took over the role of Hieroglyphics, or certainly since studies in philosophy, psychology and spirituality have encouraged the probe of self (and the universe).

In the case of this collection, it came about after a discussion with a therapist friend who lamented the fact that many of her clients were searching for the right person to make them happy. "And," she added, "some of them don't even know themselves well enough to know who or what they are looking for or what is happiness for them."

"Surely," we both acknowledged, "*every* enlightened person in this 'How to be happy' era knows that the power to bestow happiness lies within the self. But," we questioned, "who *is* the self?"

As it turned out, I discovered a good number of people who actually DO know who they are—or, in the parlance of the skeptical and/or the analytical or the hyper spiritual, BELIEVE that they do know who they are.

This question was given randomly to people with absolutely no guidelines. The way in which it was answered, was clue enough for the reader to garner insight into the writer. I *gave* it as an assignment to members of my memoir writing class, and actually, to many other people willing to get into their own heads and/or hearts and hopefully, "souls."

Several people, when asked, seemed aghast at the concept. It was not clear exactly what caused this reaction but I'm guessing: 1) they never gave a thought to defining themselves and had no desire to begin the process. 2) they were not willing to reveal themselves to "strangers," as in, "WHO I AM is none of your business." (Perfectly acceptable.)

We do understand that it is an ongoing, ever changing process, but worth the scrutiny for some people.

And then there were people who promised to do it—made several promises in fact, indicating that they were really into it, but for whatever reason—"too busy," being top of the list—left those promises lingering in midair for months and more months.

And finally—why would you, the reader, care who these people are, or think they are? For the same reason, I would suggest, that you seek out any reading material in any genre —curiosity, entertainment, relatability, insight—or you might have kin or friends or acquaintances whose work appears herein. For whatever reason, some responses you will enjoy reading, some you might want to skip, and some will remind you of something about yourself—good, bad or surprising. Happy reading!

If you or anyone you know is interested in participating in volume II of this series, please contact me.

Emily Rosen
erosen424@aol.com

A computer from the 90s.

BORN IN
THE DECADE
OF THE 1990s

- The World Wide Web launched and the Information Age arrived
- The Rodney King verdict and L.A. Riots tear the nation apart
- The WTC and Oklahoma City bombings cement "terrorism"
- Newt Gingrich redefined the American Right
- The O.J. Simpson chase, trial and acquittal
- Rap music and the new hip-hop spark debates over race
- *Seinfeld, Friends* and the new American sitcom were all about single adults
- Napster and the rise of free digital content

Loris Orsolini
b. 1990s
Future Leader

Good question.

It's a simple question for some, and a complicated question for others. It's also a deceptively powerful question.

You might ask yourself this question multiple times throughout your life. Or not at all.

The answer might change for you or stay the same your entire life.

I'm a very complicated person. My friends and family agree.

Simply put, I am ambitious. Very ambitious. My dreams are more creative than many people could imagine.

I have always had a feeling inside me that I'm supposed to do important things. That doesn't mean I'm important.

It just means I have the potential to do important things. But I know I'm not the only person.

I also love simple things.

I love being outside. At the beach, on a mountain, or in a forest. Anywhere. I love sitting and just watching the clouds go by or listening to birds.

I love to workout.

I love to read, nap, learn, meet people, be alone, etc. I know I'm not the only person.

Here' s what I've learned at 23:

1. You and I are more alike than we both know.
2. We both want the same things but how we get them is what makes us different.
3. We can change our environment by first changing ourselves.
4. Consciousness is power. Be aware of what's happening in your life and others'. If you are aware of something, you can find a solution to it.
5. Not doing something is still doing something.
6. The simple things we do and think (our habits) add up over time to either help us succeed or fail. Whether we want them to or not.
7. Willpower is overrated. You will only achieve something when you feel like your life is incomplete without it. That's what it means to truly want something.

Kierstin Geary
b. 1990s
Marketing

I am wonderfully lost in my mid-20s. While many of my peers are struggling to find themselves, their career path, relationships, and what makes them happy, I enjoy the variety of options. I have a healthy relationship with "what ifs", and I enjoy letting my mind wander to explore them. I am equally overwhelmed and content with the unknown.

I am a curious introvert who cares more about the "why" than the "what." I tend to focus on the bigger picture than the granular, and look at things how they matter in the grand scheme of things. I consider myself dependable and put my circle of friends and family above everything else.

Most of all, I enjoy knowing that the whole world is "just faking it" and that "no one has it 100% together" (some advice I've gotten numerous times in the past couple of years). It is my favorite thing, and I think we should embrace imperfection more often.

MISSING!

1970s AND 1980s
If you are one of them, contact me for volume II.

Demonstrators marched through the streets of
Chicago as the city prepared to host the
1968 Democratic National Convention.

(Photo credit: David Wilson)

BORN IN THE DECADE OF THE 1960s

- Viet Cong emerged
- US Troops to Vietnam
- My Lai Massacre
- Bay of Pigs- Cuban Missile Crisis
- JFK, Martin Luther King, Bobby Kennedy assassinated
- Johnson signed Medicare – voting rights bills
- Violence at Chicago's Democratic Convention
- Richard Nixon became president
- "The Pill" was"born"
- Marilyn Monroe – Judy Garland dead
- First heart transplant
- Beatles appeared on *Ed Sullivan Show*
- First Super Bowl
- Woodstock – 3 days of Peace, Love and Music
- Man on the Moon
- First E-mail message
- *Feminist Mystique* published

Ellen Zaroff
b. 1960s
Computer Programmer

Who are you? Was asked of Alice who replied: "I do not know sir for I haven't been myself for quite some time." I think therefore I am I am I am I am I am I am I am I Yam.

I think.

Therefore I am not. When I think, I disappear. When I think not, I am in myself whole. "What do you want?" he asked her.

She opens her mouth to speak but nothing comes out.

She looks into his eyes. Are they green or are they brown? The soft black in the center has a hazel starburst around it that explodes into aqua marine.

He blinks.

"I can't get you what you need if you don't tell me," he says. She cocks her head.

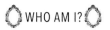
Breathe in. Breathe out. Relieve for me the weight of the world. The Atlas upon her shoulders, his burden is her burden. If he only knew how stepping onto her added to it. To be absolved of this heaviness. To have her shoulders returned and this heft off of her. Ah. To exhale and with a seismic shudder shed it and feel the wait unloaded.

Blink. Blink.

"I think tonight," she sucks in some air and then lets it go. "Some sweet potatoes would be very fine."

Lucia Leao
b. 1960s
Translator and Writer

Your invitation to write a piece about "Who Am I?" has been sitting on a shelf in my crowded, distracted mind for a few weeks. I've been pondering if that would be the right time to write about it.

Today you sent me a message stating "it is not like you to avoid such a challenge," regarding the invitation. And it dawned on me—which "you" are you talking about? Which "I" should I try to express or define?

That may be why I haven't sat down to answer that question, or to dance around it. Isn't it now totally explained? All of it?

It would be impossible for me to say something that wouldn't sound definitive, that wouldn't become definitive, in writing, in opposition to what *we*—are, could be, should be? To say we are all beings in progress would not represent the right feelings or ideas—are we advanced, advancing? To say something else would feel like trying to grasp the thickness or the lightness, the elusiveness of the air your great love breathes, around you, the night you see him/her and fall in love at first sight. I tried.

Terrence Michael Fanning
b. August 5, 1961
Bartender, Cab driver, Student, Freelance Videographer, Reformed Convict and Writer

Who Am I: is not who I once was.

I am the third of four Irish American children, born and raised in the upper part of Manhattan, Washington Heights: an Irish enclave nestled along the Hudson River with a bar on every corner. Both of my separated parents were bar tenders in the neighborhood and the taverns became the perfect forum for my fledgling shoe shine business.

When I was a boy, temperamental momma had difficulty raising four incorrigible children. She used to tell me I was an accident. Everything I touched "turned to shit." "You should've been flushed!" --malicious, detrimental words for an emotionally fragile boy. Perhaps even worse than the iron hand, belt, or broomstick. I began to believe it, and the self-fulfilling prophecy commenced.

At the age of twelve I sought refuge from an unhappy home life into the savage streets of New York City, gangs, drugs and juvenile delinquency, resulting in countless years of incarceration.

"A gun toting thug," a sentencing judge once told me. While in jail, I married Rose who was pregnant at the time of my arrest and our child was born, Nicole. We spent our first Father's Day together when she was 27, and my abandonment of her destroyed my dream of walking her down the aisle at her wedding—an emotionally crippling time in my life.

Conversely, I could be honorable, loyal and dedicated, a man with a profound compassion for people, life, love and liquor. Resolving this internal conflict has been a lifelong, tormenting process. While my body was locked up, the mind was not. I made the rehabs and prison libraries my second home, reading an abundance of classic literature, studied to get a GED and AA degree, and learned proficient Spanish. Education opened my mind to other possibilities, but I was too institutionalized and became the quintessential recidivist.

In my early thirties, after serving a four year stretch in NY, I found work as a NYC cab driver and my life changed. I met a nice woman who was renting an apartment in a swank high rise overlooking the Hudson River with panoramic views of the Palisades. We fell in love. And I met a respectable elderly doctor living three floors down in the same building. The good doctor was one of my clients. He was a patron of Carnegie Hall and introduced me to classical music. Both were major influences in my life. They tried to show me love and responsibility for well over a decade. Yet, I still could not shed the shackles of my past. And soon I returned to my nefarious ways, leaving behind the opportunity of a lifetime. I was a man of many regrets.

I moved to South Florida in 2002, shortly after the tragedy of the twin towers, which was traumatizing. I was lonely, depressed, and looking for love in all the wrong places to fill the hole in my corrosive soul. I had to be beaten into submission until 2007, at the age of 47, I finally surrendered. Not to the police this time but to a program of recovery and fellowship. I needed to be shown how to live as a free man, and the 12 steps of recovery was my journey to freedom. The spiritual awakening was not sudden. It took an army of angels to find the solution. And I began to heal from the decades of hate, violence and treachery. Acceptance was the key. Recognizing I was responsible for what I created, set me free.

In 2008, I enrolled at Florida Atlantic University as a communication major, with a concentration in film and video. With the grant money, I invested in video equipment and started a company: Legacy Video. I wanted to film other people's life stories. I saw an advertisement in the local paper for a memoir class and quickly joined. When nobody wanted their life story to be on film, I began writing about my troubled life, though I had never written a word except long letters from an alien world of confinement. There began a 10-year journey of bleeding on paper, the truth of my past. I found solace and comfort among my coterie of writers, detailing the most intimate stories of my life and other people's lives. I love my writing class.

I just returned from the world-renowned Iowa Summer Writing Festival two months ago. What an amazing experience! It was a scholarship from my fellow writers. I felt like the luckiest person in the world and determined not to screw up another "chance of a lifetime." After years of self-deprecation, I finally discovered that I am a writer who loves helping people and I volunteer as a computer instructor in my community of seniors. In fact, I recently became an advocate for my community in the battle to get their bus stops restored.

I can't change the past. It is permanent, but every day I wake up and thank God I am still alive and can be of service to those in need. After all, this is not a race, it's a marathon. It's not how you start but how you finish. I want to leave this world making a difference. A legacy of honor, dignity, and yes, Love. Today, I am a changed man.

That's who I am.

Marcie Schwartz
b. 1960s
Teacher

I AM a fireball
of vitality.
A burning life force
of dynamic energy,
powerful as the sun
lighting my way.

I AM a creative unknown.
As open as
the bluest sky,
a vastness of hope
a vision overseeing
life as it unfolds.

I AM the purity of Love
 in tender held moments.
The compassion of a
present listener,
the embrace of two
souls melding.

I AM fluid as the
changing sea.
Flowing with life,
holding nothing
and containing
everything.

I AM a force of strength.
A gust of wind breathing
life's momentum
as it unfolds
into a gentle breeze
of presence.

I AM pure joy.
Inhaling the scent of
unconditional love
emanating from
the downy crown of
my newborn son.

I AM grief.
An undercurrent of
Invisible tears beneath
a frozen stream,
flowing through life
lessons, learning acceptance.

I AM emptiness.
Invisible as air,
a soul evolving
into enlightenment
through God's grace,
as I spread my wings
And soar.

Kellie J. Falk
b. 1960s
Business Owner Executive

I'm a woman who loves a good belly laugh, doesn't brush my hair, has no regrets, lives with passion, envies women who match their accessories with their clothes, believes loyalty is first and foremost, picks purple over green regardless, is brutally honest, constantly trying to lose my damn pregnancy weight, admires those who dare to be different in a critical and judgmental world, has finally accepted my height, constantly battles not to cut my hair after a martini, has validated my religious beliefs within myself, grateful to have reached the drinking age, forgets how old I am, relieved that the monsters under my bed have moved on, appreciates the life I live and will drop the F-bomb in the most inappropriate situations. I was born a poor Mormon and I will die a rich Jew. I am also a mother who loves her sons unconditionally even though they still roll their eyes at me. And most of all I am a wife that has found her forever love in Prince Charming.

Ruby Bridges escorted by U.S. Marshals after school. The ruling of Brown v. Board of Education prompted the practice of intregration in public schools across the United States.

BORN IN THE DECADE OF THE 1950s

- Korean War
- Polio vaccine invented
- Brown vs. Board of Education decision
- Elvis Presley stardom
- Color television
- Rosa Parks refused to give up bus seat to a white man
- Fidel Castro becomes dictator of Cuba
- Princess Elizabeth becomes Queen of England
- *Cat in the Hat* published
- First man to climb Mr. Everest
- First space flight

Ivy Tomashoff
b. 1950s
Artist and Yoga Teacher

Who I Am is always changing.
The chemicals in my body. My emotions.
Where I Am. Who I Am with. What I Am doing.
I Am energy and energy moves, changes states, speeds up and slows down. Connects.
Disconnects.
I Am Everything.
I Am nothing.
Really.
I flow in and out of these feelings.
Touching the Stillness of The Present Moment. God .
Love. Peace.
Oh, when that experience of myself occurs, there is such sweetness. And.
I Am a daughter, sister, aunt and cousin. I Am part of a family. A bloodline. Heritage. Ancestors. Karma. Conditioning. Contracts.
Touching sorrow. Loss. Fear. Shame.
I touch the rim of anger and create unnecessary drama. Because.
I do not feel loved. And.
I Am a friend, teacher and student. I Am generous.
I Am kind.

I Am contemplative.

I Am soft.

I Am passionate.

I Am a student of Love.

I Am a student of Life.

And death.

Death interests me.

And astrology, art, music, and cooking. Forests, rivers, trees and oceans stir my soul in different ways from cities and museums.

And I Am moved to tears sometimes, gratitude always, for the Beauty of Everything and the privilege to add to the Peace, Beauty and Love on Earth and Beyond.

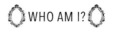

Nora
b. 1950s
Computer Programmer, Dental Assistant, Dental Office Manager, Daily Money Manager and Small Business Owner

I am a 61-year-old woman. I am compulsive and detail-oriented so the order in which I list things has meaning in itself.

I am a survivor - of emotional abuse, bullying, #MeToo, a terrorist bombing, infertility, multiple miscarriages, a late-term therapeutic abortion and several chronic auto-immune diseases. I am **NOT** a victim!

I am an immigrant. I am a student of languages and religions and cultures. I read about history and politics, murder and intrigue, romance and conspiracy. Current events and medicine fascinate me. So does time travel and science fiction. *Star Trek* over *Star Wars* any time. I carry my Nook with me always; it is never turned off and, therefore, I am never lonely.

I am a wife of 34 years to the same fascinating man. I love deeply and with all my heart. I don't believe monogamy is the only path. I do not believe that sexuality is a matter of choice. People should just be.

I am a mother of one daughter. She is a formidable woman in her own right. Her story is her own to tell. I was blessed to give birth to her and to help her grow. It's been a privilege and an honor that I don't take lightly or for granted.

I am a daughter. My parents, my younger brother and I came to the U.S. in 1965 from Argentina. None of us spoke any English. We came to find the American Dream. We did. It was hard work. There was none of that Latino pride for us; it was assimilation and belonging as soon as possible— Yeshiva for the kids so we could learn English without any ESL assistance, work for my parents as soon as they could find jobs, a house in the suburbs without any Spanish speaking neighbors three years after arrival, high school diplomas with honors and college degrees for both of us. I became my parents' ambassador to all things "American." Everything including bill paying, writing a thank you card, proofreading a business memo, writing the minutes for a lodge meeting became my responsibility. Want to know when the movie was playing? Ask me to call - the automated response was too fast for my parents to understand. Want to know what's on TV? Ask me to translate *TV Guide* listings. New insurance policy? I had to translate the coverage. On and on...

I am an orphan. I was responsible for dealing with all my parents' affairs for their entire lives. Their retirements, their downsizing to a retirement community, their health issues, and, yes, their end-of-life decisions too.

I am an entrepreneur. Four years ago, my friend and I started our business as Daily Money Managers. We assist the elderly with organizing and managing their day-to-

day financial affairs. We pay their bills, reconcile banking accounts, handle medical and insurance affairs, etc. It is very emotionally rewarding and taxing at the same time. I found great satisfaction in learning something new and in using knowledge I had gained in helping my parents as they aged.

I am me. I am trying to find myself after the responsibilities of daughter and mother are no longer priorities. Meditation and mindfulness are helping me come to live in the present. I am learning to forgive and let go of the past. I am trying not to anticipate and obsess over the future. For the first time in my life I am discovering my unique value.

Who am I? I'm changing all the time. And that's OK.

CDR
b. 1950s
Technician

I'm someone who has cared enough to save a life.

I've been a mentor several times.

I believe life is too short to deal with liars and insincere people.

I believe life is too short, period. LOL

Who am I?

I believe a person should do what makes him or her happy. I believe a person should do what he/she is able to do and make fair compensation for that work regardless of race, sex, or anything else.

I believe greed is NOT GOOD!

I believe a president should have DIGNITY (tip of the iceberg).

I believe in God, but I DO NOT believe in "organized religion."

I believe "do unto others as you would have them do unto you."

That's my religion.

Who am I?

I think, I am therefore I am...I think.

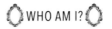

Nancy Jaslow Bader
b. 1950s
Retired Journalist and Editor
Now Teaching and Wasting Time

I am a Northern fish released into Southern waters. A 60-something Yankee journalist retired to a small town in the Deep South. I'm a glutton for fried green tomatoes but can't develop a taste for okra or boiled peanuts. I find myself saying "Yes, Ma'am" to women of all colors and ages, but I do so with a Boston accent. Seeing the remains of antebellum plantations, I understand why slavery existed, but can never condone one human's callous exploitation of another. My opinion regarding Confederate monuments seesaws between wanting to remove them because they wrongly glorify an evil chapter in our nation's history and thinking we should keep them erect as a reminder that we cannot change history, no matter how much it offends us.

When I stand, my knees snap, my neck crackles and my back pops. I've been married for 40-odd years, with no children and no regrets. I'm a two-legged mother to a pair of four-legged rescue cats. I resent people who spend thousands on purebreds when so many shelter animals need homes. I'm a writing instructor. Friend. Volunteer. I was a caregiver until my mother, disabled since I was four, died. I'm a decent joke-teller. I play tennis and play at painting. I went to college when students were protesting the Vietnam War and was a fervent liberal until I got my first paycheck and saw how much was taken out for entitlements. I naively believed that a businessman could drain the Washington swamp of waste and corruption. I still believe that a businessman can do so, just not this particular businessman.

But ask me to describe myself in just one word, and I will say, "writer." From the time I could write, I did write. Kindergarten Valentines, scribbled on red construction paper, addressed to "Mommy and Daddy" and signed with both my first and last names. Book reports, love letters, pleas from camp for canteen money and more underwear. Pleas from college for money. I had enough underwear. In journalism school, on-the-street assignments. One professor sent us out to interview the Bostonian we thought had the worst job in town. There'd be only one "A," for the student who found the best subject. I chose a trash collector. Good, but not good enough. The classmate who aced the assignment interviewed the elderly man who had tended the public men's room in the Greyhound Bus Terminal for decades, handing out paper towels and change for the ancient, permanently-stained pay toilets and cleaning up after the derelicts and businessmen who dirtied the washroom and, often, themselves. "You can learn from anyone," our professor told us. "Everyone has a story to tell."

I've spent most of my working life asking questions and writing other people's stories. My first job, straight out of graduate school, was as a cub reporter making $150 a week. I was grateful for an expense account that initially reimbursed some uptown subway rides and that later took me to Europe several times a year. It was a time of transition, from IBM Selectric typewriters to computers with floppy disks, a time when there was no "fake news." A time when the press had tremendous power, and I believed that I really could make a difference. Today, electronic and social media have shifted the priority from accuracy to speed. Get it first, then get it right...maybe. I read two daily newspapers the old-fashioned way - in hard copy. I refuse to buy a Kindle. I'm at the local library once or twice a week. I donate only to grass root causes, and my charities of choice are libraries, animal shelters and hospices. I believe that everyone should have the right to die with dignity.

I dined once with President Ronald Reagan—and 1,000 other journalists—at a White House Correspondents Dinner. I interviewed Ted Kennedy several times. As a humor writer, I won awards for finding the silver linings in the clouds of subject matter as diverse as city politics and mid-life crises.

I've written articles that earned me paychecks with two digits to the left of the decimal point. I've written annual reports that paid me five figures, with a comma. The assignments that compensated me the most weren't necessarily the most rewarding personally. I've covered everything from holes in the ozone layer to holes on the tops of men's heads. My favorite self written headline, with apologies to Shakespeare, is "Toupee or Not Toupee." Years ago, under the guidance of Emily Rosen, our class mentor, I took on my most challenging subject: me. My memoirs are a far cry from the business, lifestyle and humor writing I've done for more than 30 years.

But they've given me fresh insight into the Who, What, Where, When and, most important, Why's of my own life. I recall my college professor's adage that everyone has a story to tell. For the past 10 years, I have taught memoir-writing to seniors. Some of their stories are better than others, and some simply tell them better, but yes, everyone has a story to tell. Including myself.

I've been lucky. Katherine Graham, the late publisher of The Washington Post, once said, "To love what you do and feel that it matters—how could anything be more fun?" It couldn't be. I know.

Rene Blanco
b. 1950s
Screenwriter, author of *Fast Fiction* (Flightbooks), Therapist and Child Advocate

I'm quirky, seriously entertaining and unconventional male, in a good way despite my day job. I don't like to pay for everything but I do give away all my information and given the right circumstance, I wouldn't avoid kissing on a first date!

Never had children (that I know of, yikes), don't do strip clubs, gamble or any online sex junk but I do attend fetish parties occasionally when invited as a dancer (fully clothed)! I'm also finishing a couple short story collections for publication this year.

Politically, I'm a REALISTICAN and OPTIMISTICRAT.

Spiritually, I worship at the FIRST, LAST AND ONLY TRUE CHURCH OF OUR ONE UNIVERSAL SUPER-ORGANISM ALMIGHTY GOD.

Relationship-wise, my story is brief, my best girl passed away 5 years ago after a ten-year illness. We were tightly and lovingly united and it was a long, wonderful and inspiring relationship; I am nothing but optimistic about being part of another one just as great sometime, which was her wish too.

What I'm doing with my life?

I'm loving it! Laughing and dancing a lot. But, the reality is that saving lives and families in crisis is as difficult as any job can be, and mine doesn't pay well either yet that's what I've been doing mostly, diagnosing mental and emotional disorders, providing treatments and family therapy for disadvantaged kids and parents.

I'm really good at yoga, cooking, writing, dancing (some say), and a thousand other difficult things to do for work.

Love to eat almost anything except internal organs, and I'm wild about sauces. My favorite books are my own books, I guess I'm my own favorite writer! I also go dancing for hours at a time to good club music and live bands, I love doing that and supporting the local SoFlo music and arts scene which are hidden treasures.

Things I could never do without:

- Good health (what else?)
- Meaningful relationships (intimate/family/friends/work)
- My Projects (purposes of life)
- Recreation(beach/music/dancing/sex/HDTV/foods, and etc.)
- Spirituality (higher purpose, Higher Power)
- Money (freedom/security/earthly means/comforts)

I spend a lot of time thinking about my "next fun," my screw-ups, my accomplishments and how to get everything done as well as possible.

I like confident easy-going people, natural healthy looks, creativity, people who are mildly kinky, social and open-minded.

Nanci Sherman
b. 1950s
Lifestyle/Luxury Hotel
General and Manager Writer

I am stardust.

I am the cosmic tension between physical being and divine consciousness. I am not my body but of my body.

I am joy, fear and enthusiasm.

I have the awareness to make choice in every given moment to alter my reality.

A group of librated Jewish prisoners leaving the
Gęsiówka concentration camp during the Warsaw
Ghetto Uprising

BORN IN THE DECADE OF THE 1940s

- Warsaw Ghetto Uprising
- Mt. Rushmore opened
- Pearl Harbor attacked instigating WWII
- Allies land on Normandy Beach
- Fighting in Pacific Ocean
- Atomic Bomb devastated Japanese cities
- Germany surrendered
- United Nations founded
- First computer built
- Microwave ovens invented
- Polaroid camera invented
- Post War economic recovery

Nancy Kirschner Sinrod
b. 1940s
Lawyer and Social Worker

You asked me to answer the question, "Who am I?" I cannot give you a simple answer. The mosaic of who I am will be uncovered after I am gone. But first, who I am is being Naomi's mother. Being her mother has never been an accomplishment or a role to me. It is just a blessing.

I see now, though, that for the rest of who I am, I consist of the roles that I play in the world. I am a serious person and I have taken those roles very seriously. I am a wife. I am an eldest daughter, a lawyer, a therapist, an urban planner, an "A" student, a sorority girl, a drop-out from a sorority. I am this, I am not that. I won this, but lost at that. I am married. I am divorced. I am admired. I am rejected. I am happy. I am depressed. I am generally anxious.

I used to think that my accomplishments and failures defined my life. But no more. When did that happen? It must be very recently because I can still taste and smell what I have considered "me" when I look at my yearbooks and photo albums. I look back at the photos of me when I was young and at my daughter's childhood and think that is who I am. I made that beautiful person. But then I also think, she never belonged to me. She is her own person. She has her own mosaic. I only birthed her and gave her the wings to live her own life. Hopefully I taught her resilience and resourcefulness. Of that I am not certain. But I know I am her mother. I do know that.

Today I think that my life is made up of the tiles that construct the mosaic: my hopes, dreams and actions; my achievements and failures. The decisions I made and the decisions I did not make. Together they will compose the mosaic of who I am to be revealed in retrospect. None of my life belongs to me. It has all been fleeting and I have captured those moments only in photos and in memory. I have never been able to hang on to them. We each have our own mosaic. We each are captured somewhere.

So, when you press me and ask, well, "…where can I find this elusive you?" I am not really sure how to answer. "Who I am" consists of mercurial roles that change and reshape and then change again in dizzying fashion. You cannot find the real me in those roles because there is no real me. I am a series of different people when I am with different people on different days in different situations. I am Barry's wife when I with him and sometimes Jose's resentful ex-wife. I am the student therapist at the Faulk Center and one of the writing students in Emily's class.

So, if I am not the ever-changing roles I inhabit each day, then who am I? Well, I suppose who I am changes too. For example, this morning we went to a restaurant we go to all the time and were served by a new waitress. I was in a bad mood in the first place so when she did not come over for fifteen minutes, I was already livid and of course, when she got my order wrong I shut down and gave a mean-spirited small tip. Five minutes later, I was loving and kind on the phone to a close family friend. And then when doing an errand at the ATT store, I became impatient and bitchy again. This was all in a span of an hour and a half.

So, who am I? I can be kind and mean and insightful and insensitive. I can be impatient as well as patient, loving, caring and generous. Sometimes I am silly and immature. Sometimes I am professional and extremely mature. I can be so changeable that even I cannot keep up with all the moods and faces that I show in a day.

Also, I can talk to almost anyone and I can be a chameleon and fit into almost any social situation. When my father made friends with anyone when I was a kid, it embarrassed me no end. "Daddy, how do you know that person wanted to talk with you?" I exclaimed when we were alone. Now I do it. I will talk with anyone. And it embarrasses Naomi just as much as it embarrassed me when I was young. But I am convinced that one day she may thank me for teaching her that even a psychotic person may have something to say as significant as a sane person. And sometimes, you cannot tell which one is sane and which one is insane. And, does it really matter?

Barry
b. 1940s
Marketing Researcher for Entire Career—Employee from 1958 to 1992

I grew up in poverty in Brooklyn New York. Everyone was the same and so

I did not know I was poor until I got a part-time job in New York City.

I quickly made every effort to be successful as an adult. I had to do it on my own with no help from anyone.

I had an excellent work ethic and soon was on the road to success. My success gave me everything a person could want except "being happy."

I had a great wife and three children, a successful career, my own home and more money than I could ever dream of. My good fortune enabled retirement at age 49 and thus far 26 years of retirement.

The missing link has always been my ability to "be happy." I have never been able to understand the "why?".

My therapists across 40+ years have repeatedly said, "They would trade places with me anytime." Why can't I be happy?

I have more material things as well as really good relationships than 95% of the people in the U.S. but it is just not enough. What is wrong with me?

Maria Abesamis
b. 1940s
Zen Meditator, Community Organizer, BodyTalk Promoter, Teacher and Immigrant

Life for me began at 29 when I joined the resistance movement against a savvy 58-year old dictator in the Philippines. Shortly after, I was inducted into the communist party by a priest in the Underground. Fourteen years of fighting the infamous Marcos dictatorship shaped me into what I am now - an activist looking for any opportunity to change Bad into Tolerable Something.

In the Chinese world, where Nature is ruled by one of Five Elements, I have been defined as Fire. As a Fire person, I am volatile, passionate and desire to live Life intensely. I am curious about people, places, and experiences, and do not hesitate to speak to strangers on trains or in waiting rooms because I am forever curious about what goes on in their heads.

Because I am Fire, I am also spiritual, meaning I do not give so much value to material things as other people do, as much as to things that are unseen—the soul—if you will, people's character, their attitudes, their ways. I am always in search of secrets, what makes people feel young forever, what makes them grow, or not, or feel hatred towards others.

I am "driven" and want to make every moment count-- for how else can one make Life full and worth living? I am happiest when I'm engaged in projects beneficial not only to myself but also to others. For this reason, I have spent much time recently going to poverty-stricken Philippine communities (areas devastated by tsunamis, volcano eruptions and earthquakes, for example) where I can listen to people's stories and get healed in return. I participate in BodyTalk Outreach medical missions and encourage poor people to write their experiences, especially during the oppressive Marcos' martial law years, about which millennials and the younger generation have no knowledge. I am part of the dreamy "Never Again" movement.

Fortunately, ten years of Zen meditation following a traumatic divorce, and years of tedious caregiving to a priest - brother have made me more patient. I have learned to bite my tongue whenever I feel criticisms rising in my head. I realize I cannot change another person, so why should I stress? Why should I mess up his or her journey when it is part of a Divine Plan.

But I find it difficult to forgive. I enjoy a good banter with friends, close friends who will not twist my words or misinterpret my thoughts. I am faithful towards them and will always go an extra mile. But once betrayed or severely disappointed, I find it hard to get back on track. I am heartbroken for a lifetime and cannot tap into the old warm feelings I used to have towards my ex-. I wish I could burn away the anger, resentment, and ill feeling- but this is something I am still working on.

In love relationships, I tend to be a perfectionist. I expect "the works," an entire package of physical emotional, spiritual, psychological and intellectual intimacies to heal and comfort me. But since this is impossible, chances are that I will end up being alone. Is this such a dim prospect, I question. Or will Fire finally consume me, lift me high into the Air- higher than I can ever imagine?

Rita C. Butler
b. 1940s
Currently Retired

Is it possible that someone else might know me better than I know myself?

Undoubtedly, the project of self-definition would benefit from a degree of objectivity. But maybe I have an advantage; I know things about myself that others are not aware of. I have a feeling this should be a self-focused endeavor.

So here I am, approaching the end of my life but hopefully I will never be a finished product. For as long as I can remember, I have wanted to learn more; I've wanted to be better: more attractive, more intelligent, more altruistic and definitely more energetic. Plodding through life, always the tortoise—never the speedy hare—I've nevertheless had the satisfaction of often making it to the finish line while others ran out of steam along the way. Determination and self-discipline are perhaps my most notable characteristics I am completely at ease with ambiguity; believing, as I once read, that "if nothing is certain, all things are possible."

Too old to be a baby boomer but not young enough to be a member of Generation X, I belong to that cohort often referred to as "The Silent Generation" a period that stretches from 1925 to early to mid-1940s. My early life, growing up in one of the newly-emerging suburbs of middle-class America was shaped by the mores of that time. Gender-specific roles were outlined for me and my siblings. My sister and I were groomed for a life of domesticity. High school was considered enough education—any more would be a waste of time and might scare off a potential husband who was expecting a degree of unquestioned compliancy inherent in the patriarchal view of marriage that epitomized my parents' relationship.

In truth, I never imagined a specific career but balked at the idea of domesticity as the only possibility for my life. From an early age, I dreamed of acquiring as much education as possible and traveling, two life-long desires no one else in my family seemed to have.

While my siblings headed out to ride their bikes, climb trees and twirl on their roller skates in the driveway, I would be curled up somewhere inside reading books or creating fantasy scenarios with my dolls and doll house. An anxious child, I spent inordinate hours of every day in a state of auditory and olfactory agitation. My reactions to loud noises and strong smells were usually dismissed as "persnickety" and something I was expected to outgrow, which I never did.

In addition to being anxiety-prone, my introverted nature was complicated by an extreme case of shyness that took years to overcome. I've lived most of my life coping with a revved-up nervous system that seems at odds with my basically quiet personality.

I married very young and in one fell swoop became a wife to my husband and a stepmother to three pre-adolescent children. Overnight, I went from age twenty to thirty, at least in terms of what other people (including my husband) seemed to think I should know and be able to do. For the next forty-one years, I lived a life filled with an uneasy feeling of treading psychological waters that were over my head most of the time.

But like the steady little tortoise, I soldiered on. My husband' s work took us to the far comers of the world and satisfied my yearning to travel. My dream of an education would take longer: a BA in Languages and Linguistics at age 53, a PhD. in Comparative Studies at age 68 and an MA in Women's Studies somewhere in between, becoming the only person in my family to ever go to college. After my husband died, I became a college instructor at the Women's Studies Department at a local university.

I still love to read, mostly non-fiction, poking my way through the new-book shelf at the library at least once a week. One of my newest activities is working out at the gym. I'm as surprised at this development as my friends and family are but I like the idea of on-going challenges, a theme of my entire life. I'm no longer shy but an introvert is always an introvert and I have no problem being by myself.

I am the sole survivor of my original family. My brother and sister, both younger, have died leaving me with a feeling of loss and sadness. But my two adult sons are a big part of my life and my turtle-like self is still operative. My wide-ranging curiosity keeps me in a constant state of wanting to learn more. I'm still intrigued by people and places that are different from me.

So, WHO AM I? Someone no longer worried about the opinions of others; a person who has somehow managed to achieve all of her most desired goals and above all, someone who is grateful for what I think has been an interesting life.

'

John William Johnson
b. 1940s
Writer

I believe answering that question is as simple {or as complex) as listing what a man believes as opposed to what he's "done."

As such, 'who I am' is a man who would like:

• A world where class hatred is understood to be born out of ignorance and fear, and for us to possess the courage to act upon that understanding.

• A world where one death does diminish us all rather than get us to tune in to the 6 o'clock news to witness yet another.

• A world where time well spent isn't simply the cash register ringing.

• A world where money equals the quality of time, and not merely marking its passage.

• A world where politicians won't promise to build bridges even where there are no rivers, or to change the course of rivers in justifying the building of new bridges.

• A world where 'religion' isn't used as an excuse to judge and to classify; to maim and to kill.

• A world where we spend more time seeking to understand the questions, rather than boasting of knowing the answers.

- A world where we take individual responsibility for our actions, successes and failures.
- A world where tolerance means more than what an engineer says should be the space between two pieces of metal; indeed closing the space between ourselves.
- A world where communication among human beings is not simply a road to an end, but a highway toward new beginnings.
- A world where we understand the differences between cause and reason, thus leaving the question of "why" to never be confused by the assertion of "why not."
- A world where we understand there is no such thing as luck—luck being merely opportunity seized.
- A world where it's understood that perfection is an illusion sought most often by the inept.
- A world where there's effort to understand the questions rather than boasting of knowing the answers.
- A world where we never take less than we need; never give more than we have; never want more than we discard.
- A world where it's understood that 'connections' can open the door—followed by knowing that talent- and in a deeply committed relationship with work - is the only thing that can turn on the lights.
- A world where it's understood that a flag is a symbol of patriotism, but certainly not a measure of it; that indeed, idolatry is not what you own, but what owns you.
- A world where it's understood that we are no more than our capacities, and no less than our choices. Indeed, a world which understands there's only one choice in life—and

that choice is to, in fact, choose—which means: swim in the ocean of your choices, rather than wade in the pond of your options.

• And at the end of the day, a world where alleged activists don't manufacture facts by getting assertions Facebooked and re-tweeted—in turn and in a matter of hours those 'facts' become the 'truth' around the world for those who major in ignorance and bias at the College of Twitter and the University of Google.

ImsIms
"Baby Boomer"
Writer and Creative Manager
in the Beauty Industry

I am an artichoke: multi-layered, a little sharp and tough on the outside.

But as the leaves are painstakingly removed, a tender heart is revealed.

Though not for everyone. I believe that those who take the time to know me will be happy they did.

My upbeat, sometimes audacious exterior is just that. For inside, I am shy, lack confidence and often feel like the Wizard of Oz, hoping no one discovers my truth.

I am anxious, often fearful and insecure. I truly believe that my faults and flaws will be discovered someday and I'll be left alone and unloved. I cry easily, get angry often and try not to let my true feelings be seen...by anyone...ever.

But the good news is that I love truly and passionately. I believe I am a wonderful wife, magnificent mother and a fabulous friend! I take care of those around me with humor and caring. I am, despite my dark interior, fun to be with. I dance, play tennis, sing, write, talk and laugh. I love blonde jokes, Pinot grigio, Woody Allen movies and the beach.

I love to read and am never happier than when lying by the water with a good book! I love the sun and light. I love Christmas and I love making other people happy. I am not religious, though I envy those who find comfort and inspiration in their god.

I am vain and very conscious of my appearance, though I hate to shop, fuss with salons and try to keep personal maintenance to a minimum. (Although after 50, I became loath to leave the house without makeup!)

I am athletic, but arthritic. I dislike loud music, loud clothing and loud people. I am very neat, but despise housework. I love to cook, but hate doing the dishes. I am a perfectionist, but am aware of all that is imperfect in myself. I applaud honesty and honor it in others.

But know I can be a little sneaky if necessary! Who am I? Just like everyone else I suspect. A mass of contradictions. An enigma. A unique body of work. Perfectly imperfect.

But, at heart, like the artichoke, worth it.

Harriet Lasky
b. 1949
Major gift fundraise in Jewish Philanthropy

Country club ladies need a big tote bag to schlep around all the essential accoutrements associated with their daily life at the Club. Every tote bag should include the following items; Mahjong card, Canasta card holder, can of tennis or golf balls, whichever you prefer, and perhaps a sweater to keep the chill off in the card room. Recognizing the importance of having these items ready for use at a moment's notice, I embarked on finding my perfect country club lady tote. I didn't want the LV, Gucci, or new MCM tote, everyone has one of those. I was looking for a bag that would express the new me. I searched the web and found the perfect bag, the Tory Burch red tote. It is colorful, spacious and ready to fill with my new arsenal of equipment. Before leaving the house, I slip the bag over my shoulder. I feel liberated. Now, I'm ready to embark on my new life at the Club.

For a second, I glance back and notice my old tote standing proudly on the closet shelf. Suddenly memories of my career in marketing and fundraising come flooding back. I always had a sturdy leather bag that zipped across the top to safeguard all my valuables as I traveled throughout the city in marketing for the Ladies Home Journal and Newsweek, and as a development professional for The Anti-Defamation League and most recently American Friends of The Hebrew University. My briefcase, as I referred to it back then, included compartments for a cell phone, file folders, keys, pockets for business cards and could accommodate a pair of heels for that special meeting.

Two years have passed since my husband and I moved to sunny Florida and my magnificent country club community. I am finally ready to utter the "r-word," retirement. What I need now are new skills: how to play Mahjong, canasta, tennis or golf, and learn to relax. None of these skills are at my fingertips. I never left time to explore them in the past. My career consumed me, defined me, and gave me a great deal of satisfaction and pride. The organizations I represented had missions I believed in, "serving and preserving the Jewish communal world and Israel, defending human rights and advancing medicine and technology for a better world." Through my work, I met numerous dedicated colleagues, brilliant professors, scholars and advocates and a cadre of tremendously generous and loyal donors. These people inspired me with their devotion to service and philanthropy. I finally said goodbye to AFHU in February 2017 and decided to put my briefcase on the shelf.

Nothing in my early life prepared me for this new privileged and active lifestyle. Growing up in Boro Park Brooklyn, in a two bedroom apartment with my siblings, and Holocaust survivor parents, didn't include dinner conversations about tennis, golf or the next Mahjong tournament at the club. Life was chaotic, challenging and worrisome for my immigrant parents and siblings. My mother and father tried their best to provide for their family and make sense of their new life in America.

As the youngest child, my life was very different. I received lots of attention, love and many of the material trappings of the American way of life. By the early 1960s, my sister and brother were independent, my brother went into the Army and my sister married. I was alone with my parents. I had their undivided attention and love, but this special treatment came with a burden known to children of survivors. Your responsibility was to make your parents happy and proud at all times. You understood that to do anything less was totally unacceptable. As a loving and dutiful daughter, I did just that. I worked hard in school, received good grades, went to college, found a good job and met a really nice, red-headed Jewish law student. Barry, whom I married in 1971 and after 47 years is still my partner and best friend.

My parents gave me love, roots in my Jewish heritage and emphasized the importance of family, but their fear of the world around them and inability to overcome the hardships they endured, crept into my psyche and influenced my behavior. Barry helped me overcome my insecurities. He acknowledged the world was challenging, but with perseverance, a positive attitude and self-confidence, it offered great and exciting opportunities. I continue learning from Barry everyday about life, facts and thank him for introducing me to the beauty of our Jewish faith and traditions. Barry and I became dedicated leaders in our synagogue on Long Island, where together we embraced our commitment to Judaism and the community.

As partners in our life's journey, we raised two terrific daughters, Stacey and Brooke. Our girls fill our lives with joy and happiness. We loved watching them grow-up and change throughout the years. Now, as accomplished women, wives and mothers they have given us the greatest gift, five beautiful grand-children, Jacob (15), Gabby (12), Maddie (8), Brandon (8) and Jordana (6). Our children love coming down to Florida and sharing in the delights of our new home.

So here I am, on the threshold of new beginnings. How glorious is that! I feel excited and liberated. I welcome retirement and the new experiences and friendships it holds for me. "Oh look it's time to go," my country club ladies are waiting for me in the card room. I slip my Tory Burch tote over my shoulder and take a quick inventory of its contents. Everything is in place. I'm off.

Oma
b. 1945
Childwhisperer

I am the whisper in the night.

I am from another time, another world, another place, another galaxy. I am timeless and mindful. I am empathetic and scared. I am joyous and confused. I am alone and I am with light. I sit above but belong elsewhere.

I am a cloud, a star, a moon, a rainbow, a raindrop, a storm; I am the wind whispering, whispering, whispering. No one hears, but I do not stop whispering.

I am the flower, the dirt, the shovel, the weed, the daisy and the buttercup. I have no equal, no reality; I am timeless but not. I care. I bleed. I cry but no one sees and no one hears. I am the wind, and I do not stop whispering.

I am a rock, a stone, a boulder, a diamond but not to adorn but to contemplate.

I moan and stomp my feet, but I hide so no one can hear unless they are very still and listen for the whispers in the night. But few do.

I am the laugh, the shout, the shudder, the scream, the sigh, but few hear. I am the whisper of the night.

I am the cold, the chill, the warmth, the comfort, the one who whispers in the night.

I am daylight; I am sunset, sunrise, twilight, moonbeams, lightening. I am an angel watching over; I am watched.

I am magic. I am a moonbeam, starlight, a meteor. I am Tinkerbell. I am the whisper in the night.

I am Peter Pan, Cinderella, Snow White, and I am the Seven Dwarfs. I am the rain, the snow, the thunder, the hail. I am the sunshower.

I cannot be defined. I am the whisper in the night.

I am the fence, the gate, the door, the opening, the light.

I am a girl, a child, a woman, a creature.

I cannot be defined. I am the whisper in the night.

I am courage, I am strength, I am fear, I am joy.

I am awake, I am asleep as I whisper in the night.

A fatherless girl thinks all things possible and nothing safe.

I am a fatherless girl

I think all things possible. I think nothing safe I am undefined. I am magic dust.

I am the breath of the night; the whisper.

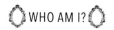

Madeline Klein
b. 1940s
Independent Travel Agent
INTELETRAVEL

917-796-2243

madeline.klein.inteletravel.com

Great question! I often wonder. I am an enigma. Changing like a butterfly. One life ending another beginning. Mostly up. Sometimes down. Reaching for the pinnacle of my success in the wheel of life. Always seems to be redefining.

In my quiet moments, I am filled with gratitude for blessings of health, family, both genetic and extended. In my heart of hearts, I know my financial edginess is present to force me and squeeze me into not settling anymore and really going for the gold which my talents can bring.

Regrets...I have my share and we keep on keeping on. All will be revealed in time

Gabriele G. Alexander
b. post WWII
Globe Trotter, Interior Designer,
Artist and Physical Fitness Trainer

A profound question, surely not easily answered by many. Although I consider myself extremely observant, a trait I polished since childhood, I have to admit that I never asked myself this question.

It would be easier to tell who I am NOT.

I will no longer qualify at any sports in the Olympics, be a Playboy centerfold only because of that darn belly fat, or be a Victoria Secret model strutting my skimpily clad bod in stilettos down the runway wearing angel wings.

It takes guts to confront yourself in trying to uncover who you truly are. Getting naked in front of a mirror and really looking deeply into your soul? Scrubbing away the camouflaging make up and dusting powder? Seeing your face with all its imperfections void of lip gloss? Although that might not be enough.

Well, I do know who I am. And I am very proud of who I am. And how I have morphed into this incredible fabulous woman. I never had the urge to justify or explain ME to others.

Our cellophane society has become more plastic; we look but do not see. I could embellish and even expand on my accomplished positive persona and nobody would be the wiser and get away with it. People who have temporarily walked along my path with me never showed an iota of desire to establish a relationship or build history with each other here in Florida.

Florida, the land of palms and sunny, sandy beaches and mandatory air conditioning must have plunged their thermometer of compassion into the lower digits.

They will never know that I conduct monthly gatherings of intimate groups of single women over sixty to help them downsize their emotional baggage, teach them about the healing powers of homeopathy, update their hairdo and convince them not to continue their never-ending drama of widowhood fifteen years in the making, and still milking it. And wear monochromatic patterns and ditch their girdles.

I might even succeed convincing a few, eventually, to pull the cumber band with golden filament reduced to dust, from the mothballs and toss it. The one their husband had worn with great discomfort on their wedding day fifty years ago, and hated it.

I am a full-fledged and hot blooded Scorpio woman, BRAVO, last water sign in the Zodiac and final day before it turns into Sagittarius, thank goodness.

And with Venus swirling above my crib, I was endowed with lots of special goodies to the envy of many.

Once upon a time I was the girl all mothers wished their sons to marry. I became a real pro in dodging their doting because marriage never made my dream list. Their sons were not of the caliber I desired to challenge or channel my lust and enthusiasm for life.

Even at a young age I never fit a contemporary mold or danced within the chalk lines drawn by strangers or society.

I am my mother's daughter. I am eternally grateful to her that she had paved a solid foundation brick by brick for me to grow into this spectacular woman. I miss her each and every day. I am sad she never saw me walking on sunshine under a rainbow after the storm throughout my life.

I look into the mirror and see a reflection of perfection, ignoring the multitude of sunspots, wrinkles and the nasty inches around my waist that had appeared out of nowhere without my permission.

I know who I am. And I love being ME.

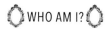

Jan
Leo, 29/11
b. 1940s
Free Spirit

My essence is ever changing—I am a seeker, a person curious about the world and my place in it. As I learn and grow in consciousness, I try to change to be more effective, peaceful, healthy. I see no end to this journey to wholeness— when I leave my current body, I will continue my quest.

David Wainland
b. 1940s
Sculptor, Writer and Poet

A rumpled wrinkled man, bearded and grey, dressed in faded jeans, single pocket tees and worn sneakers, I transverse this world leaving behind a dusty record. My hands are callused, worn and unrecognizable to me, beaten by years of fire and forge, marked by age.

I will leave behind a heavy blue folder of stories, memoirs, poems, and sketches. A record of my life for my family and the family of my family to wonder about.

My mark on the world is my sculptures. Creations of iron and acrylic paint. A prolific artist whose works are spread across the country, for good or bad, my legacy.

I've shared in tragedy, victory, jealousy, and love, coming out, in the end, a simple rumpled, wrinkled man taking on life and winning.

BORN IN THE DECADE OF THE 1930s

- Hitler elected in Germany
- Clarence Birdseye invented frozen food
- Empire State Building opened
- Lindbergh baby kidnapped
- German atrocities recognized
- Franklin D. Roosevelt elected president for the unprecedented first of four terms
- New Deal offers new job programs to combat The Great Depression
- Devastating dust storm in South Dakota
- First Master's Golf tournament in Augusta, Georgia
- Social Security Act passed
- *Gone with The Wind* published
- Golden Gate Bridge opened

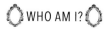

Dave Hejum
b. 1936
Engineer

I have honed my skills in the last five years while living at a Home for Seniors. A daily brisk walk around the perimeter and in its center have made me familiar with numerous items of interest which are not quite up to par. Using my senses of sight, smell, feel and hearing I have been able to detail items needing maintenance. This is not the maintenance usually applied i.e. repair or replace but that of attention at first signs of wear. I have compiled numerous lists of items which need to be treated by schedule when deterioration is imminent.

A list of various items will allow you to see the need:

The walk we use; slabs with coloration differences including paint spillage, large winding cracks and bad matches one to another which creates dripping/falling;

A fountain at the Home's entrance which sucks water from a base and shoots 6 or more feet high except when plugged by leaves or the wind blowing the water away from the intake. The exception creates water which modulates less than 1 ft. high and looks very silly;

White colored markers indicating direction for vehicles to follow are fading. They wear to ½ or more before they are attended.

The furniture we use; some cracks but primarily fading of sealer as to appear ready for the junk yard;

Some 200 bulbs encased by a plastic hood at all the elevators. At least 30% need repair continually due to heat from the bulbs;

Elevators with growing thumping noises on start and stop;

Elevator interiors with gashes and holes cause by carts long waiting for repair;

Four car-park doors in repair on average of one each at all times enticing stray people to walk in without approval;

Wall pictures hung crooked and never seem to be noticed;

Painting of various rails along walls where tape was not used to ensure straight lines;

Pruning of bushes and trees is delayed beyond the time specified and results in shabby appearance;

Repair for the items above have had requests made but receive delay notes from a number of maintenance people for a number of reasons. The most frequent seems be a lack of belief in a timely system. I have received the title "NIT PICK" from some residents. i.e. Paying too much attention to petty details. So be it. I will continue to advise the use of true maintenance and consider these last five years as valuable to producing a much-improved appearance of our Home.

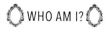

Irene Kessler
b. 1930s
Opera Singer and Psychologist

I am angular, twinkling, growing, sunny, dark, flowing, straight out, solid and sensitive all according to the day and sometimes the hour of that day. I am all these things and more.

I am a mother, grandmother, friend, psychologist, singer, actor, director. I've had many jobs, too many. But right now my main job is taking care of myself.

At the moment I am plumbing the depths of me to uncover secrets. I know the answers are in there, in my memory bank, somewhere, allusive, hiding, afraid to show themselves. I survived it all, so why is it so difficult to open it up, bring it to the light.

Which part is need at this very moment? The angular with its sharp points digging in? The sunny growing and twinkling to avert falling into a pit of depression? The flowing part that allows me to be creative?

I never know which will show itself. Which will take over and dictate my day. It doesn't ask for permission. And I—I have to deal with what shows up and allows all the different emotions to show themselves.

You see, I'm writing my memoir.

Billie Solomon Cohen
b. 1931
Teacher, Special Ed and Remedial Reading

O wad some power the giftie gie us
To see oursels as ithers see us.
-Robert Burns

So you ask, "Who am I?" Now? I am certainly not the same person I was when I was 20, 45, 65. Hell, I'm not even the same person I was a few years ago. I hardly recognize myself anymore, so little of past Me remains. And I'm not just talking about the physical 95 lbs. that's left.

I was a different person at different times, or stages of life. To name a few that stand out in my mind: a college student, a young widow, a wife and mother of young children, a teacher, a mature woman (whatever the hell that means), a free spirit.

Then there's the ME as seen by others. As a young child I was told I was a *vildeh chayeh*, a wild spirit (or less lovingly, wild animal.) My first-grade teacher thought I was more of a handful than two little boys; my mother had to accompany me on any class field trip. I was a little hyper, something, I acknowledge, that lasted in part through much of my adult life. (Even now, it remains as a bit of impatience.) I only had brief glimpses of who others thought I was. (See quote above.) Phrases, labels and comments like, "you're so talented" and "you're so clever" always surprised me and felt…I don't know…inappropriate…off the mark. I did very well in school but never felt exceptional in any way. Whatever I did, others could do better. What I had was energy, determination, and patience for the task at hand, however impatient I was with others. My mother understood that about her *vildeh chayeh* and taught me to knit, crochet, and embroider at an early age, for which, even now, I am so grateful.

Of course, there was the Me as defined by my relationship with others. First, I was Al and Anne's daughter. Briefly, I was Earl's Cohen's widow; I was George Cohen's wife for a very long time. "Oh, you're Barbara's mother, Ellen's mother." I clearly remember the day that my cat Mike and I were standing on the front step of our house in Mt. Vernon, when a neighbor walked by and said, "Oh, you're his mother!" That was the day I decided I needed to get a job. (Okay, that didn't really define me but it shows how we're seen.)

These are the traits that have been at the core of me all my adult life. I am caring of people and animals, I share easily, offer help readily; I'm vain; I'm impatient; I like order, beauty and graciousness. I am thrifty but spend easily on art; I am charitable. What do YOU see that I left out?

So now, as I finish my 87th year, I am definitely an Old Lady. Young men offer me seats on buses, help me on stairs. Looking back at all those other personas, I am not dissatisfied. Some parts of me I'm pleased with, some things I wish I could do over. I have come to an acceptance of life at this stage less special than I had earlier dared to imagine. No doubt, others see me differently. T'was ever thus.

Deborah Blanchard
b. 1930s
Consultant and Human Resources

Who am I? Really? My first thought was, who cares who I am and then the gray cells turn the question around and thought, "Well you made it into your eighties, take the challenge and run with it."

So who am I? I am a person, like so many other women, who is someone's daughter, someone's lover, someone's sweetheart, someone's wife, mother, grandmother and etc., just to name a few. However, that really tells anyone who is reading this absolutely nothing about who I am. Have you stop reading yet? I would have.

No doubt I am a product of my life experiences. I have made poor choices along with serious mistakes but there has also been learning lessons from those mistakes. Unquestionably there are events that have come about in my life that have brought me great happiness. I had nurturing parents growing up, a profession I was good at and a husband, the second time around, who is supportive, loving and after 54 years of marriage I am still very much in love with.

Congratulation if you have gotten this far. Shall I continue?

What happens when we are not needed full-time in those

roles I have mentioned above? For me it was when I reached middle age. Like many women I had spent much of my life nurturing others, being what other people wanted me to be, but spent very little effort nurturing myself. Once I started the process of making that transition and took time to reflect and look back on my life, all of the doubts and confusion did not come from not knowing who I am, but came from secrets and issues I had not dealt with. I never lost myself or my core values along the way. Whatever trauma I was experiencing there was always enough of me to eventually find my way out.

An unexpected positive outcome happened once I started to share those secrets with my husband and family. All of my life I had tried to be that perfect daughter, perfect wife, perfect mother never recognizing that trying to be perfect has its limitations, repercussions and a ripple effect on people you love. That came into full bloom when I was having a conversation with my daughter and after I finished sharing an important event she looked at me and said, "Oh my God mama, you are human after all."

I am now a complete human being who has total freedom to be who I am.

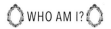

Lois A. Weisman
b. 1930s
President of Board of Directors of the Faulk Center for Counseling, Boca Raton, Florida

I am a thread that weaves through a complicated, colorful woven fabric called life: trying to maneuver through the various patterns and loving and helping to guide my family and friends with my experiences. Sometimes it's treasured and other times not. Always making sure that the thread doesn't break. Carefully. As my thread goes in and out, it pulls in different directions. So, do I.

As my fabric starts to reach its completion, I hear my mother's voice softly guiding me to always be a kind, loving, empathetic, peace maker, accomplishing my goals, and to make a difference. BUT most of all to be satisfied.

Renée Kass
The age of consent

Who Am I?

I am a Gemini! (Ying/Yang)

I am Perfect! (If I have flaws, I don't know what they are.)

I've had a wonderful life, filled with great people.

I've also had trauma, disappointments, toxic people and loss.

I'm a positive thinking person (at most times).

I enjoy being social and I enjoy being with me.

I can be alone but never feel lonely.

I have a new perspective in life; I sold a big house, and I have a great apartment.

Got rid of responsibilities–new found freedom.

I am blessed to have wonderful friends. (Yep, got rid of the toxic ones!)

I have a Generous Spirit and Kind Heart (to those who deserve it).

Integrity, Loyalty and Accountability are of the utmost importance to me.

There have been relationships that have been made and lost because of these traits.

With all this Perfection, I am also a "work in progress."

All in all, I am a Very Blessed Lady.

And that my friends = Perfection.

Steve Kates
b. 1930s
Ad agency maven in NYC, then COO
of Fit American Deerfield Beach until
retiring in 2000,
Film Critic and Feature writer for Boca
Raton *OBSERVER* for 10 years, and
Subsequently, Board member and
Memoir Writing Instructor at the
Institute for Learning in Retirement in
Boca Raton

After nine years and hundreds of thousands of dollars for psychoanalysis, one would think I'd know myself. Perhaps I did, when that particular therapy had concluded. But that was almost forty years ago.

Who I am today is quite different. The passage of time, good and bad life experiences, and a mercifully fluid perspective have conjured up a new self, a self I'm satisfied, even happy, to claim as the real me. And herewith, I will try to define WHO I AM.

Bernard Berenson, no mean intellect himself, divided people into categories of life enhancing or life diminishing, which I find a pretty impressive and accurate measuring barometer for evaluating ourselves and others.

Brilliant (180 I.Q.), erudite, witty, multi-talented, well-educated, charming, somewhat curmudgeonly, I consider myself a life enhancing force. I am also (still) hair-trigger tempered, judgmental, seemingly cold to outsiders, and excessively and sometimes unjustifiably acid tongued.

In defense of a more inclusive self-portrait, I am a fiercely loyal and appreciated friend to a small coterie of wonderful men and women, a proudly loving husband, the father of two incredible children, and the beneficiary of the love of four extraordinary grandchildren, smart, beautiful, engaging and personable - everything I would wish for emanating from my gene pool and my wife's.

Events leading up to my current self-satisfied state were not always pleasant. My early childhood was a Byzantine blend of love, harsh discipline and loneliness. I have suffered (endured?) the effects of a somewhat traumatic youth with skillful denial and fortitude; only now, at 82, have I realized the futility of sustaining past resentments and I have finally relinquished them to my great relief.

I prefer privacy, and then small groups of friends —I dislike, and am frightened in large groups, particularly of strangers. As an only child, I discovered solace and escape in reading; it was there that I discovered worlds more accommodating and felicitous than my own privileged but unhappy reality.

I am spontaneous, generous, humorous, and empathetic. I love the children in my family with an uncompromising fidelity, but I generally dislike young children out of my immediate orbit – they are irritating, noisy, ill-mannered, poorly behaved and, generally, unattractive (to be fair, there are exceptions).

The more interesting inquiry would be, "How do others perceive me?" By my very nature, I admit I am biased. I suspect that many of the characteristics I've put forth herein would re-surface. I shudder to contemplate ones I've omitted but that others see as glaring flaws. Those people are probably misguided, but are entitled to their opinions.

The wonderful thing about being 82 is that I no longer care one whit what they think of me. How I see myself, how I appreciate what I am, warts and all, is what matters now.

WHO AM I? I am a good and happy man.

Helaine Gari
May 18,1931
Fashion Retail/Personal Shopper/ Management
Associate Degree: Early Childhood Education

I am a woman of fortitude.

I am a woman who has stubborn streak which I refer to as tenacity that has served me well at taxing times.

I am a woman who is cautious, living a conservative lifestyle but liberal in thinking.

I am a woman who possesses a strong sensuous side with a love of the arts, and take pleasure in surroundings which please my senses.

I am a woman who loves books which captivate my imagination and stimulate my mind.

I am a woman who enjoys people but has just a few very close friends.

I am a woman who is independent and co-dependent, delights in social interaction but is also happy to be alone.

I am a woman who is a "nitpicker" and has been accused of micro-managing because I need order and routine to keep me comfortable. Change is not easy for me.

I am a woman like many others who have had challenges

but none that I have not been able to overcome especially with the help of others who I call my "angels."

I am a woman who has been blessed and thankful with gratitude for the woman I am.

Sonia E. Ravech
b. 1936

Over the years, I have worn many hats including that of medical assistant, administrator, office manager, teacher and homemaker; however, the job of which I am most proud is that of wife, mother and grandmother.

Often, when I walk through my community admiring all the luxurious homes, I try to imagine the families who live inside. The one with imposing lion statues flanking either side of the entrance probably houses a CEO of a powerful corporation. The family who lives in the house with the figurines of two fairies perched atop a blue gazing ball in their yard most likely has a whimsical spirit. The owners with a large statue of an angel, arms outstretched, hovering over the ferns and geraniums, must be spiritual individuals who look to the heavens to keep their home and loved ones safe.

When I look at the frontage of my own Mediterranean style home with its manicured landscaping, elegant white fountain and abundance of colorful begonias, I understand that the guessing game I have been playing, is just that…a game. Life is far too complicated to assume to know the people who live behind closed doors by the façade they display to the public. The external trappings of my life do not reflect who I truly am.

Although I live in a prestigious country club community,

I am not a participant in the country club lifestyle. I do not play cards, Mahjong, golf or tennis, preferring to participate in educational classes, lectures and workshops. I also contribute my spare time to charitable endeavors. I am the past president of my synagogue, Temple Ohabei Shalom in Brookline, Massachusetts, and am a member of several charitable organizations volunteering my home for fund raising events.

I rarely participate in country club functions and only occasionally eat at the club, preferring to cook and entertain at home. The interior of my house, although spacious, is not adorned with ornate columns, carved crown moldings or excessive accessories, but rather reflects a comfortable, contemporary elegance with plenty of open floor space, little clutter and numerous photographs of my family adorning the walls of every room. As a perfectionist, I choose to do my own housekeeping.

Although my closet is filled with more clothing, shoes and purses than I need, my outfit of choice is slacks, a tee shirt and clogs. Shopping is not a pastime I enjoy. I shop if I need something or spot a bargain. I'm not impressed with designer labels. I rarely wear makeup or jewelry.

I enjoy gardening and being surrounded by the sights and sounds of nature. I appreciate the arts, ballet, opera, theatre and leisurely browsing through museums. I can be brought to tears by a haunting melody played on a violin or the poetic language of a well-crafted novel. I am an avid reader and enjoy writing about anything and everything: my family, current events, places I visit and observations of people I encounter.

I strive to earn respect from my friends and acquaintances by being a thoughtful person because I truly believe "kindness is its own reward." My family is my priority. I love every child, grandchild and great grandchild unconditionally, even when they disappoint me, and only when I'm asked do I offer my advice, trying not to be judgmental.

Lest I sound pretentious, I am well aware I have flaws. I talk too much. I am impatient with imperfection in both myself and others. I need to be realistic of my expectations. I'm not tolerant of messiness. I'm not motivated to get into better physical shape, although I know it would improve my health. I realize alcoholism is an illness, but I have no sympathy for those who choose to drink and drive. I abhor rudeness, vulgarity and individuals who blow their automobile horns without provocation. I also have difficulty forgiving those who are abusive or mean to either humans or animals. However, I try not to let my short comings define me. If I had to choose one word to describe myself, it would be "optimist."

Some would say it is easy to have a positive attitude when you are surrounded with good fortune. I'm sure that is true, although I've met people who are not happy despite all their luxuries. I am extremely blessed to have financial security as well as healthy children and grandchildren, but I have not escaped my share of adversity. I was raised in poverty because of a father who was a chronic gambler. My troubled childhood included being the victim of an anti-Semitic attack; an encounter with a pedophile; serious confining illnesses; and an abundance of responsibilities.

As an adult, I suffer from arthritis and chronic back pain and have survived several serious surgeries. I've faced the estrangement of my youngest sister; the murder of my only brother; the deaths of my parents and husband; as well as the disappointment of having a grandson I rarely see and a son who has struggled with drug addiction. My faith, accompanied by my understanding that there are always others worse off than I, has gotten me through these trying ordeals, allowing me to maintain my gratitude and optimism.

I am an eighty two year old woman, mother of four, grandmother of seven, great grandmother of two and widowed after sixty two years of marriage. I truly cherish life, with all of its challenges, and I thank God every day for the privilege.

This is who I am, this my true identity.

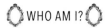

Dorothy Polayes
b. 1930s
Artist and Volunteer

I am a woman. That is not as simple as you might suppose. Yes, I am a female, with all the expected physical parts, but I am much more than that. I have a brain. I think. I possess understanding, perhaps wisdom. I have a lifetime of experiences. Many have been positive, and of those, some have been remarkable. I have emotions. I feel things deeply but I have learned to steel myself against being easily hurt or offended. Mostly, I succeed but there are some cases in which the hurt lingers and will not fade away. Still I keep trying! I hope I behave in such a way that I never hurt or offend another person.

I truly believe that "man is a social being". I enjoy people. I relish the conversation, the things I learn from others and how those things may affect me. Always, I try to remember to be sensitive to the feelings and opinions of others. For that reason, I choose not to deal with controversial topics. I still abide by my mother's cautionary words, "If you can't say something nice, don't say anything." I like to share my experiences with others, too. There are so many stories to share and I especially like to relate stories with a bit of humor. I generally see the bright side of things. So much of what we feel about our lives depends on our perspective. I'm realistic. I don't use rose-colored glasses, but I do truly believe that how we handle obstacles and unpleasant truths has a profound effect on our own well-being. If I think positively, I'm the one who benefits most.

I am a mother. When I was in my twenties and thirties, my children came first in my daily routine. I recall one day while playing in my weekly ladies bridge game, my older daughter, Faye, came home from school and I stopped, momentarily, to ask how her day went. My very dear friend chastised me for holding up the game. My answer was swift, "My children come first." All four of us intertwined in many ways. All of us were involved in the Sisterhood of our Synagogue and one after another served as Sisterhood President. We were friends as couples, too. Every week, each of the four players put five dollars plus our winnings into the "kitty" and every few years we had enough funds to spend a weekend in New York and once to go to London for a week. Obviously, things were a lot less expensive back then.

I tried hard to be the best mother ever. Did I succeed? Certainly, I am blessed with two wonderful daughters and I hope it was because of me and not in spite of me. I love being a grandmother to my one grand-daughter but I regret that I was not able to see more of her as she was growing up. I now have a great-grand-daughter, three months old as I write this. New Haven, CT., where they live, is far from Delray Beach, but thanks to Instagram, I see how she is developing day by day. It lifts my heart each time I see a new picture. I enjoy sharing them with my friends but I don't to overdo it. I don't like to brag, but I confess to having two of the brightest, most accomplished daughters, very different, and, each in her own way, very productive. Both are now retired, as are their husbands, (am I really that old?) but certainly not inactive.

I was a devoted wife to my husband, Ben, whom I married, three days after I graduated from Vassar College, having just turned twenty. Our marriage lasted almost 63 years until his death, after a rather long decline. He was almost 32 when we married, and represents my entire adult life. We sometimes laughed when we recalled that he started college the same year as I started kindergarten. He was as devoted to me as I was to him. He and his brother, Jack, started a business a few months before we married, using as start-up money, $400, which Ben gave him. It was all he had left after buying me a lovely engagement ring and his brand new stream-lined car. We certainly weren't rolling in dough, but I never felt deprived in any way. I've never felt that I needed more than I had. I never tried to keep up with the neighbors who might have had a larger home, a fancier car, or more cashmere sweaters. The business grew, became international, but never large, until it was sold to a small conglomerate in 1985 for a handsome sum. That money, carefully and conservatively invested has grown to a sum I could never have imagined, has enabled us to live well, travel all over the world and to enjoy sailing on our own ketch, just the right size for a crew of two…us!

Ben's success, and our conservative investing, most of which I handled, since Ben didn't want to be involved, have left me able to do something that has always been important to me, and which I learned at an early age from my parents' example, and that is to give. It is said that when you give you get back more in return. I have a good feeling resulting from what I have been able to do thus far.

For the past 20 plus years, I have had the pleasure of, first studying and then working in soft pastel. I have had a number of solo and group art shows, won a number of awards and have made many sales, although I've never worked at marketing my work. That hasn't been a major goal.

Finally, I hope I am a good friend. I certainly try to be. I try to be helpful, to be considerate of others' needs even in small ways. I hope I succeed in that respect. So, what am I? A good woman, a self-confident woman, a creative woman, a doer. After all of the above, I'm just me and hope to remain so.

Sandra Chatelain
b. 1939
Product of NYC Schools, Brooklyn PS 104 and PS 259, RN, LCSW, and CAP

I am a spirit currently incarnated in an aging white female body of reasonable dimensions and excellent, though not perfect, health. I am a being evolving in consciousness. Philosophically I am an admirer of the teachings of Buddha and Jesus but have no current center for communion or worship with other like-minded people. As I age, I see more clearly the desirability of getting off of the wheel of birth and death: Nirvana. Since I know I am not evolved to the point of liberation, I wish for wholehearted willingness to be *bodhisattva*, to get my lower self out of the way. It is good to be preoccupied with wishing for the good of all beings everywhere and with behaving with merit.

I am bookish but undisciplined. If there is value in astrology, I am consistent with my birth sign. We are reputed to be great starters but poor finishers, often losing interest in things once the basics are mastered. I maintain interest in people, however. I care about what happens to them and stay in touch. I don't forget people.

I have a strong histrionic streak which I sometimes wish had been more cultivated but I recognize that it could have nourished my ego to dangerous proportions. It was used in the service of others during my career. I enjoyed a reputation for making complicated topics clear in my capacity as counselor and instructor. I miss that part of my work most. I love an audience when I am "in the flow." I particularly enjoyed teaching inmates and see myself somewhere in the continuum from Ma Barker to Mother McRee.

I am a "connector" of people who need to find each other and a conduit of information. By some synchronicity, I file away a piece of information that someone needs to know shortly after I acquire it. It pleases me to pass it on or to see the connection between people take place.

I am blessed with the sense of humor that often accompanies growing up in a shaky household. I prefer to see the horrible humor in difficult circumstances. If I don't laugh, I'll cry.

I am a coward in some situations, reluctant to march as an activist, for instance. I am very mindful of my wish to keep my teeth in my mouth. That wish feeds my cowardice. Because I am in recovery, I am attentive to the temptations to pride, lust, anger, greed, gluttony, envy and sloth. In the past, I recognized greed and envy as my salient defects but am now more inclined toward gratitude for the recognition that I have enough and am enough. The envy is of people with great long-term marriages. Time is running out on that one. I am more judgmental than I would like to be. I deeply believe Jesus when he says, "Judge not lest ye be judged." I aspire to be a person who leaves people feeling good, about themselves and about life.

Genetically I am 31% Western European, 23%

Scandinavian, primarily Western Norway, 18% Finnish/ Northern Russian, 15% British and 12% Irish/Scots/Welsh. That adds up to 99%; nothing there to explain the intense obsession with dancing, especially to Latin rhythms, that has dominated my social life. I have made ability on the dance floor more important than character more than once. If given a choice to attend a networking, career-enhancing event versus an opportunity to dance at an event to which all the dance hall hotshots were invited, well, so much for networking.

The body I inhabit is allergic to alcohol. Given my ethnicity, that is not a surprise. The Swedes were the first to prove the heritability of alcoholism. My family tree is decorated with shot glasses and gossamer garlands of delusions of grandeur.

Other than all that, I am a mass of carbon-bonded atoms that is host to billions of bacteria, most of them friendly. I believe they and I and you, dear Reader, are One.

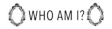

Louise Mirkin
b. 1930s
Retired Editor

Imagine a cubist self-portrait—angles, distortions, layers—done in charcoal, black, gray, and white. That was me, a self-portrait I created in a college art class. I thought of myself then as a puzzle with pieces that didn't fit together. It has taken me a long time to feel like a whole and integrated person—years of psychotherapy and life experience to figure out who I am, what I want, how to be me.

I believe the circumstances of my childhood stifled my personality and suppressed my emotions to the extent that I became introverted, submissive, and influenced by the expectations and opinions of others. In a different environment, I might have evolved into who I am now without the obstacles and struggles I had to overcome.

Although I have never been or wanted to be an actress, I've played many roles in my life depending on my relationship with the most significant person at the time—my mother, my father, a teacher, a boss, a boyfriend, a husband, a girlfriend. I tried to be whoever they wanted me to be, to please them and win their approval. This tendency also contributed to my delay in discovering who I really am.

It's difficult to describe myself as I am now at age 78

without comparing myself to earlier times and without saying what I am not. I am self-reliant, compassionate, supportive, grateful, and content. Now retired, I am more of a people person than I was during my professional editorial career, when I interacted with people only for business purposes. Empathy was not required.

As a volunteer facilitator in a mental health counseling center, I can identify with the clients because of my own experiences with depression and bipolar disorder. I am generally tolerant of other people's idiosyncrasies mainly because others have had to be patient with mine. I am competent in certain areas, like editing and proofreading, and inept in others, like sports and singing. I am strong in handling major crises, like death or illness, but easily annoyed by minor irritations. In other words, I may overreact to a computer glitch but remain calm and controlled when a loved one is in hospice.

I often felt out of sync with my peers, who were married and raising children, while I was single and focused on my job. It was important to me to be self-sufficient and independent. However, I was married twice and amicably divorced both times, and I was childless by choice, never wanting to be responsible for anyone else—not even a pet.

After 35 years of full-time work in Chicago, I retired and reinvented myself. Unencumbered by a job and a husband, I moved to Florida, where I have made a good life, comfortably and quietly living with Peter, my long-time companion.

Two months before my 70th birthday, I received a kidney transplant, the most significant happening of my life, and I am very grateful to be stable and healthy.

I believe that experience, when I was recuperating and Peter was taking care of me, solidified our relationship. He reminds me that he is the grateful recipient of my tendency to be other-directed.

Today all of my pieces fit together nicely, and I would paint my self-portrait as an impressionist, soft in tone but vivid in color.

Ruth H. Fader
b. mid-1930s
Salesperson, Classroom teacher, Homeschool Teacher Business owner and Volunteer

"I am what I am and I look like what I look like." I love that attitude, those words from Mrs. George McGovern when her husband was seeking the office of the Presidency of the United States.

It took me a very long time to grow up. As I aged, I held on to many habits and actions that should have been left behind in my adolescence. Why regression instead of progression? Oh, if I could only turn that clock back, how I might have changed things. Of course, I faked being a grown-up but inside I knew that I had a long way to go before I was there.

Faking it seemed to work for me. Something inside of me made it important for me to be liked which, of course, is very telling. I was popular in high school and college, a caring and financial aid to my husband as he studied to become a veterinarian, a teacher for five years and a mom to a son and two daughters.

And then, it was fate, serendipity, "bashert," that sent me to a neighbor's home in the fall of 1974, to borrow butter for cookies that I was baking for my youngest daughter's Brownie troop. I don't remember any other time that I borrowed from a neighbor but certainly it was fate that brought me to that spot. My neighbor and I got into a discussion about tourism in our home town (Baltimore) and the fact that there was nothing available for visitors to see the city, no tour buses, no tour guides. I had recently taken a trip to London and had fallen for my tour guide so our talk hit a point of interest. The discussion that day about touring in Baltimore turned into a wonderful adventure and a very successful business partnership which lasted for thirty-one years, until I sold the company in 2005. I feel as if I "birthed" a baby and that offspring is out there, growing and flourishing.

When your plate is full, when decisions must be made, when people are dependent on you, when family matter are overwhelming...growing up is no longer an option. It's a must! And so, I worked to make my company expand, to help my children grow into responsible adults and to support my husband as his physical being took a hit. Might I have done things differently? Maybe. But, at the time, I was doing my best to be a loving daughter, a devoted wife and mother and a caring "boss."

"And so, Miz Scarlett, I grew up." It's been a great journey and although it took me a while, to get there, it was surely worth it. As well-known author, Philip Roth said in an interview in early 2018: "I go to sleep smiling and wake up smiling. I'm very pleased that I'm still alive. Moreover, when this happens, as it has, week and week, month after month since I began drawing Social Security, it produces the illusion this this thing is just never going to end, though of course, I know that it can stop on a dime. It's something like playing a game, day in and day out, a high stakes game, that for now, even against the odds, I just keep winning. We will see how long my luck holds out."

As for me, at age eighty-two, I consider myself very lucky. Life is like a roller coaster, full of ups and downs. I try hard to keep up, up, up. My mantra...ATTITUDE and GRATITUDE.

Rhoda Rubenstein*
b. 1937

"Who am I, but the stories I tell and the ones I believe to be true."

Daughter, wife, mother, lover, sister, aunt, friend, writer and woman. These are the categories that identify me.

Teacher, English language specialist, job counselor, tester and evaluator, rehabilitation specialist, business owner and private "eye." These are the careers I have pursued.

Italy, Paris, Russia, China, Australia, South America, Turkey and the United States. These are the places I have traveled.

Brooklyn, Queens, Long Island, California and Florida. These are the places I have lived.

Who am I?

Special, ordinary, compassionate, giving, friendly, tender, angry, sad, loving, kind, vengeful, hopeful and content. These are the windows to my soul.

Who am I?

What defines me?

I am my memories, but who is left to share my memories? Just the people to whom I will tell my stories.

"Who am I but the stories I tell and the ones I believe to be true."

*DECEASED 3-23-2019

International Film Service

SPEAKER GILLETT SIGNING THE SUFFRAGE BILL

The bill providing for a Constitutional Amendment granting the suffrage t
women throughout the Nation was signed, as shown above, by the Speaker o
the House of Representatives after it had been passed by the Senate

BORN IN THE DECADE OF THE 1920s

- League of Nations established (and closed)
- 19th amendment passed giving women the right to vote
- Quota system established curbing legal immigration
- First Miss America Pageant
- Construction begins on Yankee Stadium
- First issue of *TIME* magazine
- Warner Brothers Incorporated
- First "talkie" movie
- President Harding dies in office—Coolidge takes over
- IBM founded
- Teacher John Scopes convicted for teaching theory of evolution
- NBC radio network founded
- Lindbergh pilots first non-stop trip from N.Y. to Paris
- Worst stock market crash in the U.S. history

"The Wizard of Is"
93 years young
Retired Rabbi

The words for "I am" in French are *je suis*. You will note that removing the "I", it becomes Jesus.

The time has come to put the "I" back in Jesus and know that He is who You are and I AM.

When Moses climbed Mount Sinai and asked God His name, He replied: "I AM THAT I AM." When I ask myself the same question I get the same answer: I AM THAT I AM.

I am the balance point between my spiritual self and my material self. My spiritual self has been materialized and my material self has been spiritualized. I am the god that you are and you are the god that I am. I am that I am. I am not my appearance. I am not my personality, I am the mighty, I am presence. I am the ubiquitous one. There is no one that I meet that I am not. I am not who I think I am. I am who I am willing to be. I am before Abraham was.

Hal Spielman
b. '20s
Market Research Business Executive
and co-author of Suddenly Solo

As compared to last year when I was only 89, things seem different now that I'm 90.

For example: People who know I am 90 want to do things for me, partially because they now think of me as old so they make efforts to keep me seated. "Let me do that" is their common refrain at almost anything requiring me to move, stand, walk, reach, or lift.

Of course this also impacts on my mind set as to what I can and cannot do.

For example: Last year I opened the dining room table to its full extent to seat 12 people. But as I approached the pulling of leafs to do it once more, I said to myself, "Wait till the kids get here and they will do it." After all, I am 90.

Last year at 89 I climbed the two step kitchen ladder/stool to change a light bulb. But this year, I demurred. After all, I am 90.

Last year I was kind of hesitant about wearing my hearing aids. But now I wear them more brazenly. After all I am 90.

Also have you noticed how easily the "9" and the "0" come to hand on your keyboard?

There seems something defining in the exclamation point that is the number "90." Am I dumber, certainly less active, perhaps a bit slower, or less self-reliant than at 89? Maybe. Certainly friends and family treat me as if I am. And maybe that's not so bad. After all, I am 90.

Gloria Shapiro
b. September 28, 1923

The other day a friend asked me to answer the question, "Who Am I?" Some friend! Only a sneaky provocateur would ask such a question. Nevertheless, I've decided to turn a critical eye on this creature I've been living with for ninety-five years and see what comes up.

First, the easy part—the façade. Anyone who cares to look would find a short lady with a good bosom and waistline, more than ample hips and legs of no distinction whatsoever. It's a figure better suited to the long skirts and bustles of another era. Oh well, one must work with the merchandise at hand. I suppose you might say, as a saving grace, I'm not a bad looker—hardly beautiful, mind you—but a smile does work wonders.

So much for the superficial. Now let's take a peek at what's lurking beneath. It's a mixed bag, as I suspect it is for most of us. Let's be positive and start with the good stuff.

The heart, as important emotionally as it is anatomically, seems in pretty good shape. It is loving and caring—at the ready to run with chicken soup for a sick friend. Family will always be the special place I tap into for the nourishment that supports my life and soul.

I was born nosy, although I prefer to think of it as being

blessed with curiosity. I want to know about everything. Well, maybe not everything. It does exclude whatever touches, even tangentially, upon math. I don't give a fig about isosceles triangles or the intricacies of $E=MC^2$. I'm not at my best with abstractions.

I know how to make a friend and keep a secret. You stack up lots of brownie points for that. A friend needs to know you're not a blabbermouth. I find a really good book can be as exciting as a lover's embrace—although a few years ago there might have been some argument about that.

Anyone within earshot will agree that I have strong opinions and am not shy about expressing them—politics, euthanasia, does God exist and why tattoo—any of them will do as opening gambits for discussion. (I may mock the idiots who deface their bodies with hearts and curlicues but will defend to the death the idiot's right to do so.) See what I mean? Some might see me as a judgmental prig but better to enter the fray than sit wishy-washy on the sidelines.

I still think I'm pretty open minded. That requires listening, really listening, and as much as I like to talk, (no argument there) the other side of the question does deserve a proper hearing. Prejudice raises its ugly head everywhere and I'm working hard to slay that particular dragon. Right now I'd rate myself a B—maybe a B+ on a good day—but A is the goal. I've always aimed for the A. I'm told I project an air of confidence—the kind of person you 'd ask to recommend a decent doctor.

An adventurous spirit is a gift—and mine is all decked out with perky pink and purple ribbons. I've explored a fair bit of the world and hate that my ancient knees are yelping about doing more. However, as long as the mind can fly free I hope to keep soaring over the Alps, the Pyramids and New Jersey. Sadly, I've given up on climbing Mt. Everest— and giving up does not come naturally to me. Instead, I'm trying to make do with the lure of untried Ethiopian food, the Times crossword and other kinder, more gentle pursuits

I'm not mean or petty, don't bear grudges, give short shrift to whiners and despise dishonesty. I have a live and let live attitude for all things that move—well, maybe not cockroaches or those pesky little ants that run crazed in all directions on my kitchen counter.

I cannot live without the arts. Can't sing a note, draw a straight line or dance a mazurka and am properly awed by those who can. Outsize talent will always find me appreciative— and more than a little jealous. The coloratura hitting her high C with the ease of cracking an egg makes me wish it were me up there showing off my abilities. Having beauty in my life is a non-negotiable requirement. Sometimes, even the purple bougainvillea sprawling outside my window will do.

Toss into the mix a decent sense of humor and a soupcon of two of my favorite words in the English language— generosity and passion. I know I can be over enthusiastic at times, but dead fish responses speak to me of a soul that's starving to death.

With such wonderful traits I've made myself sound like quite a prize, haven't I?

Unfortunately, there's another side to the coin. I must admit to a flourishing ego that's in a shooting war with ever present doubts. Little red men with pitchforks and horns delight in pricking my vanity, reminding me of my failings and reveling in my discomfort. Just when I think I've handled a situation well, up pops one of these tiny monsters and whispers in my ear, "You could have done it better." The greater my uncertainties, the more I overcompensate with a show of confidence that can make me sound like a know-it-all.

Okay, I admit I'm far from perfect but the road to improvement begins with awareness, so my mea culpas go like this. Every January my New Year's Resolutions begin with, "You will not be so damned judgmental!"—but by April somehow that commitment has lost its urgency. When patience was doled out, I was out to lunch—a very long lunch. I plead guilty to being a bit of a snob and do not suffer fools lightly. That doesn't prevent me from exchanging a juicy bit of gossip now and then. In fact, if the pickins are good it can sweeten up a dreary day.

My tachometer is always on high as if getting there before the fire engine was some great virtue—wherever there is. I have a temper (it's not for nothing that I come from Hungarian stock) and if you can't be on time for a date, after the third or fourth offense the guillotine awaits. Happily, the anger doesn't linger.

I worry a lot. What will people think when I dressed in pearls and should have worn jeans? Thankfully, as I've grown older I worry a lot less about what people will think. Kicking and screaming I've been dragged into the technology age and am convinced that every miracle device was invented just to aggravate me. I am not brave about change.

So there you have it, the good and the bad of it. I notice I've devoted nine paragraphs to my virtues and only four to my less attractive traits. Have I tried to skew the image? Well—probably. But age has its perks so perhaps I'll be forgiven for wanting to put a rosy shine on things.

I wish I could have painted a more exotic picture. It would have been good to mention my adventures in the Peace Corps or let drop that I was once the toast of Broadway. None of that happened. It's been, after all, just a little life. I have tried, though, to squeeze every last bit of joy out of it and somehow managed the sorrows that came uninvited to my doorstep. What's evolved from the long, challenging, exciting, curious, shattering, chaotic and absolutely gorgeous journey is—me.

I'm not finished with life yet and I hope life isn't finished with me. I still have things to do. The juices are flowing—well, some of them, anyhow, and I haven't stopped dreaming about possibilities. What's more, I dream about them in glorious Technicolor. None of that dull black and white stuff for me.

So, in the end, "who am I?" Perhaps a flawed but fairly decent specimen who bumbles along each day trying to do better. As for the rest—I'll think about that tomorrow.

I've loved working. I started out on the faculty of Rutgers University and mention that first because it sounds impressive. I hate to add I was there only for a year and left to get married. In 1947 who was thinking women could do it all? After the kids got a head start, I worked as an Interior Designer for 25 years and enjoyed exercising my creative genes. After retirement I returned to my first love—theater. Actually, a sort of theater. I've been a professional lecturer and book reviewer in Florida for over 20 years and am still writing and performing. The ham in me loves it and you have no idea how encouraging it is to receive a paycheck at 95.

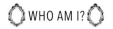

Emily Rosen
b. 1927
Writer, Editor, Teacher and Counselor

I am a very lucky—as in winner of the good life lottery—90+ year old work in progress. Not a day passes when I don't learn something new about me, about you, about the way the world works. Most important in my life is the fact that I have learned the difference between reasonable expectations and realistic ones and have taught myself to live with realistic expectations. Therefore, I am rarely disappointed, hurt or angry.

I live with ups and downs and plateaus. My ups come from putting words together and reading the words of other people, from the sun, from flowers, (even fake ones) mountains, oceans and forests, from short change-of-venue trips ,(and happy return home from them) from reminiscing about past travel and other experiences, from the sounds of birds, human voices, musical instruments and timely silences, from people in my life, from hugs and touches. from cooking and home entertaining, from riding my bike, from driving my yellow car, and from a bunch of "stuff" I don't understand.

Since widowhood, in 2013, I have discovered the joy of living alone, of complete independence, of the feathery lightness of having no one dependent upon me, and the joy of making and breaking plans without having to do so in consultation with anyone else. I appreciate the blessed serenity of aloneness and my freedom to choose when to be with people—and to choose the ones with whom to "be."

My downs come from things I cannot control and I try to give them little of my consciousness. When they occur, I own them and the feelings that "come with."

Plateaus are my stability and I have learned to embrace them with joy because I am never bored. I am never bored because I am happy when my mind is at rest and empty, and happy when I am engaged in my mind-dialogue. I lead a life of balance between stuff cerebral and stuff mindless.

I'm a strong believer in "giving back."

I like myself. I don't dwell on my flaws, (of which there are many) on my health, or my imminent demise.

I believe football is a metaphor for what's wrong with this country. I distain people who don't educate themselves about candidates and issues and who don't vote. I avoid crowds, and that includes restaurant meals with more than two other people. I prefer one-on-one "dates" with friends.

I dream of a clean desk.

I do not define myself by my progeny—all of whom I love dearly—and feel loved by.

I am not a leader nor a follower. What people think of me – is, (because I love this cliché) none of my business. If someone had not written "the serenity prayer," I would have done it myself. I am the sum of my belief system, the pillar of which is humanism. My daily mantra is simple: be careful and be grateful.

Estelle Berman, M.A.

b. 1929 (so not fair)
National Certified Counselor and Certified Professional Coach

When I was young and my mother old, she said to me, "When I look in the mirror an old lady looks back at me, but there is a young person still inside me. That young person still has dreams and wishes." Now that I am looking in the mirror, I understand because that old lady is in my mirror. The young person in me is trying to escape. Who I am today, is someone doing a balancing act. How much can I still dream and wish for, and how much will the mirror lady stop me? What is realistic for me to believe I can still do? Today, this minute in time, I win, and know I can still be productive. It will be difficult, but I cannot blame the mirror lady. She is not my totality, I am separate from her in many ways.

Carol

b. 1927
Counselor, in School Systems, Facilitator of Private Groups and Library Volunteer

I am not the person I once was and in the short time remaining as my future, I doubt I will recapture my former self.

So be it! When you are hit on the head with a sledge hammer, very few of the pieces "Cohere."

Fortunately, or not, I still think, therefore I am.

About the Author

"Why did I do this?
I'm still trying to figure it out
Some questions have no answers
Sometimes, the answers to
questions are deeply hidden
Sometimes, you just gotta go with
the flow."

B.A.- Journalism and Marketing–M.A.–Education–and–M.A. Special Ed. M.S.–Mental Health Counseling.

Various jobs in advertising, publishing, teaching at all levels, freelance feature writer, and columnist, "Everything's Coming Up Rosen"–see website below.

Owner of successful singing telegram company, "Witty Ditty"–and then a personalized poetry company, "Pryme Rhymes".

Since 2000–instructor of writing workshops–MEMORIES, MILESTONES AND MEMOIRS and editor of two anthologies of stories from my classes. Political Junkie–former Board member of League of Women Voters (Palm Beach County).

Volunteer and Group Leader and former Board Member of Faulk Center for Counseling (Boca Raton, Florida).

Many other volunteer experiences. Adventure traveler–occasion biker. Ever mindful.

Website: www.emilyrosen424.com